Pocke Keeping your Kids Safe Online

A Practical and Concise Handbook for Parents

NATHALIE VAISER, CEH

Contents

Chapter 1: The Importance of Keeping Kids Safe Online

Introduction

As more and more of our daily lives take place online, it's essential that parents take steps to ensure the safety of their children while they are using the internet.

One of the first steps in keeping kids safe online is understanding the landscape in which they are operating. This includes knowing what platforms and apps are popular with kids, as well as the potential risks and dangers that exist on those platforms. Common online platforms and apps used by kids include **social media, messaging apps**, and **online gaming sites**. These platforms can provide a wealth of educational and social opportunities for kids, but they can also expose them to cyberbullying, online predators, and other potential risks. **Later in the book you'll find guidelines on adjusting privacy and other security settings for a variety of platforms,** including **Facebook, TikTok, Instagram, Snapchat, WhatsApp, Roblox, Minecraft,** and **Fortnite.**

To help kids stay safe online, it's important for parents to establish boundaries and rules for their use of the internet. This can include setting **limits on screen time**, establishing **age-appropriate restrictions**, and establishing **rules for online behavior**. For example, you might set rules about what types of content kids are allowed to access, who they are allowed to interact with online, and how they should conduct themselves while using the internet. **You'll find in this guide a list of apps for iPhones, Android phones, PCs and Mac computers to help you with parental controls.**

Another important aspect of keeping kids safe online is **educating them about internet safety**. This can include **teaching kids how to protect their personal information**, such as their name, address, and phone number, and discussing the dangers of **cyberbullying** and how to respond if they encounter it. It's also important to teach kids how to **spot and avoid**

online scams and fraud, and to be aware of potential predators who may try to lure them into dangerous situations. **There are free online courses that are mentioned later in this book.**

To help parents keep track of their kids' online activities and protect them from potential risks, there are also a variety of **parental control and monitoring tools** available. These tools can allow parents to set age-appropriate restrictions, block inappropriate content, and monitor their kids' online activities. It's important for parents to research and understand the different options available and choose the tools that best meet their needs and the needs of their kids.

Despite our best efforts, there may be times when kids encounter problems or dangers while they are online. It's important for parents to know **how to respond** in these situations, whether it's dealing with **cyberbullying**, **inappropriate online behavior**, or other issues. This can include taking steps **to report the incident** and **seeking help from appropriate authorities**, as well as talking to kids about the incident and helping them to understand and learn from the experience.

Chapter 2: Understanding the Online Landscape

As children and adolescents spend more and more time online, it's important for parents to understand the various platforms and apps that they are using. This can help parents to better navigate the digital landscape and make informed decisions about how to keep their kids safe while they are online. Detailed below are steps you can take to secure each of these applications and online sites to better protect your child's privacy.

Security Guidelines for Popular Online Platforms and Apps

Social Media Platforms

Social media platforms are among the most popular online destinations for kids. These platforms allow users to create profiles, connect with friends and family, and share content such as photos, videos, and updates about their lives. Below are some of the most popular social media platforms and recommendations to use configure them for best privacy and safety.

Facebook

One of the most well-known social media platforms, Facebook allows users to connect with friends and family, join groups and communities, and share content such as photos, videos, and updates. Facebook is popular among kids and teens, but it has a minimum age requirement of 13.

- Set privacy settings: Facebook offers a range of privacy settings that allow you to control who can see your child's profile and posts. Encourage your child to use these settings to limit the visibility of their profile and posts to friends only, or to a specific list of friends.

- Use the "Friend" feature carefully: Encourage your child to only accept friend requests from people they know and trust in real life. Remind them not to accept friend requests from strangers.

- Monitor your child's activity: Regularly check in on your child's Facebook activity to ensure they are not engaging in risky or inappropriate behavior.

- Educate your child about online safety: Teach your child about the potential risks and dangers of the internet, including cyberbullying, sexting, and predator threats.

- Use parental controls: Consider using parental controls or monitoring software to help protect your child from inappropriate content and activities on Facebook.

Instagram

A photo and video-sharing platform, Instagram allows users to post and view pictures and short videos, as well as interact with others through likes, comments, and direct messaging. Instagram is particularly popular among younger kids and teens.

- Set privacy settings: Instagram offers a range of privacy settings that allow you to control who can see your child's profile and posts. Encourage your child to use these settings to limit the visibility of their profile and posts to friends only, or to a specific list of friends.

- Use the "Follow" feature carefully: Encourage your child to only follow accounts that they know and trust in real life. Remind them not to follow accounts that seem suspicious or that post inappropriate content.

- Monitor your child's activity: Regularly check in on your child's Instagram activity to ensure they are not engaging in risky or inappropriate behavior.

- Educate your child about online safety: Teach your child about the potential risks and dangers of the internet, including cyberbullying, sexting, and predator threats.

- Use parental controls: Consider using parental controls or monitoring software to help protect your child from inappropriate content and activities on Instagram.

TikTok

A social media platform focused on short-form video content, TikTok allows users to create and share 15-second videos set to music. TikTok has become particularly popular among younger kids and teens in recent years.

- Set privacy settings: TikTok offers a range of privacy settings that allow you to control who can see your child's profile and posts. Encourage your child to use these settings to limit the visibility of their profile and posts to friends only, or to a specific list of friends.

- Use the "Follow" feature carefully: Encourage your child to only follow accounts that they know and trust in real life. Remind them not to follow accounts that seem suspicious or that post inappropriate content.

- Monitor your child's activity: Regularly check in on your child's TikTok activity to ensure they are not engaging in risky or inappropriate behavior.

- Educate your child about online safety: Teach your child about the potential risks and dangers of the internet, including cyberbullying, sexting, and predator threats.

- Use parental controls: Consider using parental controls or monitoring software to help protect your child from inappropriate content and activities on TikTok.

YouTube

YouTube is a video sharing platform that allows users to upload, share, and view videos. It is one of the most popular websites in the world.

- Set up parental controls: YouTube has built-in parental controls that allow you to restrict the types of content that your children can access. You can enable these controls by going to the "Restricted Mode" settings in your account settings.

- Create a separate account for your children: Consider creating a separate Google account for your children and setting their account to "Child" mode. This will allow you to set stricter controls on the content that they can access and will also enable other features such as the ability to set time limits on their device usage.

- Monitor their viewing habits: It's important to regularly check in on what your children are watching on YouTube. This will allow you to catch any inappropriate content that they may have stumbled upon and discuss it with them.

- Use the "Pause Watch History" feature: YouTube has a feature called "Pause Watch History" that allows you to pause your children's watch history from being saved to their account. This can help to prevent them from being recommended inappropriate content in the future.

- Educate your children about online safety: It's important to teach your children about online safety, including the importance of not sharing personal information with strangers and being careful about what they click on. Encourage them to tell you if they come across anything that makes them feel uncomfortable or unsafe.

Messaging Apps

In addition to social media platforms, kids also use messaging apps to communicate with friends and family. These apps allow users to send text, video, and audio messages, as well as make phone and video calls. Some of the most popular messaging apps used by kids include:

WhatsApp

A messaging app that allows users to send text, video, and audio messages, as well as make phone and video calls. WhatsApp is popular worldwide, including among kids and teens.

- Set privacy settings: WhatsApp offers a range of privacy settings that allow you to control who can see your child's profile and posts. Encourage your child to use these settings to limit the visibility of their profile and posts to friends only, or to a specific list of friends.

- Use the "Contacts" feature carefully: Encourage your child to only add contacts to their WhatsApp list that they know and trust in real life. Remind them not to add contacts that seem suspicious or that they do not know well.

- Monitor your child's activity: Regularly check in on your child's WhatsApp activity to ensure they are not engaging in risky or inappropriate behavior.

- Educate your child about online safety: Teach your child about the potential risks and dangers of the internet, including cyberbullying, sexting, and predator threats.

- Use parental controls: Consider using parental controls or monitoring software to help protect your child from inappropriate content and activities on WhatsApp.

Snapchat

A messaging app that allows users to send text, video, and photo messages that disappear after they are viewed. Snapchat is particularly popular among younger kids and teens.

- Set privacy settings: Snapchat offers a range of privacy settings that allow you to control who can see your child's profile and posts. Encourage your child to use these settings to limit the visibility of their profile and posts to friends only, or to a specific list of friends.

- Use the "Friends" feature carefully: Encourage your child to only add friends to their Snapchat list that they know and trust in real life. Remind them not to add friends that seem suspicious or that they do not know well.

- Monitor your child's activity: Regularly check in on your child's Snapchat activity to ensure they are not engaging in risky or inappropriate behavior.

- Educate your child about online safety: Teach your child about the potential risks and dangers of the internet, including cyberbullying, sexting, and predator threats.

- Use parental controls: Consider using parental controls or monitoring software to help protect your child from inappropriate content and activities on Snapchat.

iMessage

A messaging app that comes pre-installed on Apple devices, iMessage allows users to send text, video, and audio messages, as well as make phone and video calls. iMessage is popular among kids and teens who use

Apple devices.

- Set privacy settings: iMessage offers a range of privacy settings that allow you to control who can see your child's profile and messages. Encourage your child to use these settings to limit the visibility of their profile and messages to friends only, or to a specific list of friends.

- Use the "Contacts" feature carefully: Encourage your child to only add contacts to their iMessage list that they know and trust in real life. Remind them not to add contacts that seem suspicious or that they do not know well.

- Monitor your child's activity: Regularly check in on your child's iMessage activity to ensure they are not engaging in risky or inappropriate behavior.

- Educate your child about online safety: Teach your child about the potential risks and dangers of the internet, including cyberbullying, sexting, and predator threats.

- Use parental controls: Consider using parental controls or monitoring software to help protect your child from inappropriate content and activities on iMessage.

Online Gaming Sites

Online gaming sites are another popular destination for kids. These sites allow users to play games, often with other players, and may also include features such as in-game chat and messaging. Some popular online gaming sites used by kids include:

Roblox

A gaming platform that allows users to create and play games, as well as interact with other players through in-game chat and messaging. Roblox is popular among younger kids and teens.

- Set privacy settings: Roblox offers a range of privacy settings that allow you to control who can see your child's profile and messages. Encourage your child to use these settings to limit the visibility of their profile and messages to friends only, or to a specific list of friends.

- Monitor your child's activity: Regularly check in on your child's Roblox activity to ensure they are not engaging in risky or inappropriate behavior.

- Educate your child about online safety: Teach your child about the potential risks and dangers of the internet, including cyberbullying, sexting, and predator threats.

- Use parental controls: Consider using parental controls or monitoring software to help protect your child from inappropriate content and activities on Roblox.

- Report inappropriate behavior: If your child encounters inappropriate behavior on Roblox, encourage them to report it to the platform. You can also report the behavior yourself through the Roblox website.

Minecraft

A sandbox-style game that allows players to build and explore virtual worlds, as well as play with others online. Minecraft is popular among kids and teens of all ages.

- Set privacy settings: Minecraft offers a range of privacy settings that allow you to control who can see your child's profile and messages. Encourage your child to use these settings to limit the visibility of their profile and messages to friends only, or to a specific list of friends.

- Monitor your child's activity: Regularly check in on your child's Minecraft activity to ensure they are not engaging in risky or inappropriate behavior.

- Educate your child about online safety: Teach your child about the potential risks and dangers of the internet, including cyberbullying, sexting, and predator threats.

- Use parental controls: Consider using parental controls or monitoring software to help protect your child from inappropriate content and activities on Minecraft.
- Report inappropriate behavior: If your child encounters inappropriate behavior on Minecraft, encourage them to report it to the platform. You can also report the behavior yourself through the Minecraft website.

Fortnite

A battle royale-style game that allows players to compete in large-scale multiplayer matches. Fortnite is particularly popular among younger kids and teens.

- Set privacy settings: Fortnite offers a range of privacy settings that allow you to control who can see your child's profile and messages. Encourage your child to use these settings to limit the visibility of their profile and messages to friends only, or to a specific list of friends.

- Monitor your child's activity: Regularly check in on your child's Fortnite activity to ensure they are not engaging in risky or inappropriate behavior.

- Educate your child about online safety: Teach your child about the potential risks and dangers of the internet, including cyberbullying, sexting, and predator threats.

- Use parental controls: Consider using parental controls or monitoring software to help protect your child from inappropriate content and activities on Fortnite.

- Report inappropriate behavior: If your child encounters inappropriate behavior on Fortnite, encourage them to report it to the platform. You can also report the behavior yourself through the Fortnite website.

It's important for parents to be aware of the various online platforms and apps that their kids are using and to understand the potential risks and dangers that may be associated with them. By staying informed and taking steps to protect their kids, parents can help to ensure their children's safety while they are online.

Potential online dangers and risks

There are many potential dangers and risks associated with the online platforms and apps used by kids. Some of these risks include:

Cyberbullying: One of the most common risks that kids face online is cyberbullying. This can include things like mean or threatening messages, harassment, or the sharing of embarrassing or private information.

Cyberbullying can have serious consequences, including low self-esteem, depression, and even suicide.

Online predators: Kids may also be at risk of encountering online predators, who may try to lure them into dangerous or inappropriate situations. These predators may use social media, messaging apps, or other platforms to try to establish relationships with kids and gain their trust.

Inappropriate content: Kids may be exposed to inappropriate or explicit content while using the internet, whether intentionally or accidentally. This can include things like pornography, violence, or hate speech, which can be harmful or disturbing for kids to see.

Scams and fraud: Kids may also be at risk of falling victim to online scams or fraud. These can include things like phishing scams, in which perpetrators try to trick kids into giving out personal information, or fake online stores or contests that ask for payment or personal information.

Compromised personal information: Kids may also be at risk of having their personal information compromised while using the internet. This can include things like their name, address, phone number, or other sensitive information that could be used for identity theft or other nefarious purposes.

To help protect kids from these and other risks, it's important for parents to be aware of the potential dangers and take steps to educate their kids about internet safety and to use parental controls and monitoring tools as appropriate.

Chapter 3: Setting Boundaries and Rules

One of the key ways that parents can help to keep their kids safe online is by setting boundaries and rules for their internet use. This can include setting limits on screen time, establishing age-appropriate restrictions, and establishing rules for online behavior.

Setting Limits on Screen Time

One of the first things that parents can do to help keep their kids safe online is to set limits on screen time. This can help to ensure that kids are not spending too much time on their devices and are engaging in other activities as well. There are a few different ways that parents can set limits on screen time, including:

Setting specific time limits: Parents can set specific time limits for how long kids are allowed to be on their devices each day or week. For example, you might allow kids to have one hour of screen time per day, or a maximum of three hours on weekends.

Setting daily or weekly schedules: Parents can also set daily or weekly schedules for when kids are allowed to be on their devices. For example, you might allow kids to use their devices for an hour after homework is done, or only on weekends.

Using parental control tools: Many devices and internet service providers offer parental control tools that allow parents to set limits on screen time. These tools can be used to block access to certain apps or websites at certain times of day, or to set limits on how long kids can use their devices.

There are several ways to limit screen time on an iPhone:

- Use the "Screen Time" feature: The "Screen Time" feature, which is built into the iPhone's operating system, allows you to track your device usage and set limits on the amount of time you spend on specific apps or activities. To access this feature, go to "Settings," then select "Screen Time."

- Use the "Downtime" feature: The "Downtime" feature allows you to set a specific time period during which only phone calls and approved apps will be available on your device. To access this feature, go to "Settings," then select "Screen Time," then select "Downtime."

- Use the "App Limits" feature: The "App Limits" feature allows you to set limits on the amount of time you spend on specific apps or categories of apps. To access this feature, go to "Settings," then select "Screen Time," then select "App Limits."

- Use parental controls: If you have children, you can use the "Family Sharing" feature to set limits on their device usage and restrict access to certain apps or content. To access this feature, go to "Settings," then select "Screen Time," then select "Family Sharing."

By using these features, you can effectively limit screen time on your iPhone and help ensure that you are using it in a healthy and balanced way.

Limiting screen time on an Android phone

There are several ways to limit screen time on an Android phone:

- Use the "Digital Wellbeing" feature: The "Digital Wellbeing" feature, which is built into the Android operating system, allows you to track your device usage and set limits on the amount of time you spend on specific apps or activities. To access this feature, go to "Settings," then select "Digital Wellbeing."

- Use the "Wind Down" feature: The "Wind Down" feature allows you to set a specific time period during which your phone will switch to grayscale mode and only phone calls and approved apps will be available. To access this feature, go to "Settings," then select "Digital Wellbeing," then select "Wind Down."

- Use the "App Timer" feature: The "App Timer" feature allows you to set limits on the amount of time you spend on specific apps or categories of apps. To access this feature, go to "Settings," then select "Digital Wellbeing," then select "App Timer."

- Use parental controls: If you have children, you can use the "Family Link" feature to set limits on their device usage and restrict access to certain apps or content. To access this feature, go to "Settings," then select "Digital Wellbeing," then select "Family Link."

By using these features, you can effectively limit screen time on your Android phone and help ensure that you are using it in a healthy and balanced way.

Setting Age-Appropriate Restrictions

In addition to setting limits on screen time, it's also important for parents to establish age-appropriate restrictions for their kids' internet use. This can help to ensure that kids are not accessing content that is not appropriate for their age or development level. Some things that parents might consider when setting age-appropriate restrictions include:

Blocking inappropriate websites or apps: Parents can use parental control tools or browser settings to block access to websites or apps that are not appropriate for kids. This can help to prevent kids from accessing explicit or harmful content.

Setting age limits on social media and other platforms: Many online platforms have age limits, which can help to ensure that kids are not accessing content or interacting with others that are not appropriate for their age. Parents should be aware of these age limits and make sure that their kids are not using platforms that are not suitable for their age.

Monitoring kids' online activities: Parents can also monitor their kids' online activities to ensure that they are not accessing inappropriate content or interacting with others in inappropriate ways. This can include monitoring their kids' social media accounts, messaging apps, and other online activities.

List of Phone Monitoring Applications

Here are several popular phone apps that parents can use to monitor their child's activities:

Qustodio: Qustodio is a parental control app that allows parents to track their child's online activity, set limits on device usage, and block inappropriate websites and apps. It is available for both iOS and Android devices.

OurPact: OurPact is a parental control app that allows parents to track their child's device usage, set limits on app usage, and block inappropriate websites and apps. It is available for both iOS and Android devices.

Kidslox: Kidslox is a parental control app that allows parents to track their child's device usage, set limits on app usage, and block inappropriate websites and apps. It is available for both iOS and Android devices.

Net Nanny: Net Nanny is a parental control app that allows parents to track their child's online activity, set limits on device usage, and block inappropriate websites and apps. It is available for both iOS and Android devices.

Kaspersky Safe Kids: Kaspersky Safe Kids is a parental control app that allows parents to track their child's online activity, set limits on device usage, and block inappropriate websites and apps. It is available for both iOS and Android devices.

By using these apps, parents can monitor their child's activities and help ensure that they are using their devices safely and responsibly.

Establishing Rules for Online Behavior

In addition to setting limits on screen time and age-appropriate restrictions, it's also important for parents to establish rules for their kids' online behavior. This can include things like:

Teaching kids to protect their personal information: Parents should teach their kids to be careful about sharing their personal information online, including their name, address, phone number, and other sensitive information.

Discussing the dangers of cyberbullying: Parents should also teach their kids about the dangers of cyberbullying and how to respond if they encounter it. This can include telling kids not to engage with bullies and to report any bullying to a trusted adult.

Establishing rules for online interactions: Parents should also establish rules for how their kids should interact with others online. This can include things like not talking to strangers, not sharing personal information with others, and not engaging in inappropriate or harmful behavior.

By setting limits on screen time, establishing age-appropriate restrictions, and establishing rules for online behavior, parents can help to ensure that their kids are as safe as possible online.

Chapter 4: Educating Kids About Online Safety

One of the key ways that parents can help to keep their kids safe online is by educating them about internet safety. This can include teaching kids how to protect their personal information, discussing the dangers of cyberbullying and how to respond, and providing tips for spotting and avoiding online scams and fraud.

Teaching Kids to Protect Their Personal Information

One of the most important things that parents can do to help keep their kids safe online is to teach them to protect their personal information. This can include things like:

Not sharing personal information online: Kids should be taught not to share their personal information online, including their name, address, phone number, and other sensitive information. This can help to prevent identity theft and other problems.

Using strong passwords: Kids should also be taught to use strong passwords for their online accounts and to change them regularly. This can help to prevent unauthorized access to their accounts.

Being cautious about sharing personal information with others: Kids should be taught to be cautious about sharing personal information with others, even if they seem trustworthy. They should be encouraged to ask a trusted adult for advice before sharing personal information online.

Free Courses for Children on Online Safety

There are several free online courses that teach children how to be safe online, including:

Google's Be Internet Awesome: Be Internet Awesome is a free, interactive course designed to teach children about internet safety, security, and responsible online behavior. It is available for both iOS and Android devices. Website: https://beinternetawesome.withgoogle.com/

Common Sense Media's Digital Literacy and Citizenship Curriculum: Common Sense Media's Digital Literacy and Citizenship Curriculum is a free, online course that teaches children about internet safety, security, and responsible online behavior. It is available for both iOS and Android devices. Website: https://www.commonsense.org/education/digital-literacy-and-citizenship-curriculum

International Association of Computer Science and Information Technology's Online Safety for Kids: The International Association of Computer Science and Information Technology's Online Safety for Kids course is a free, online course that teaches children about internet safety, security, and responsible online behavior. It is available for both iOS and Android devices. Website: https://iacsit.org/online-safety-for-kids/

Federal Bureau of Investigation's Internet Safety for Kids and Teens: The Federal Bureau of Investigation's Internet Safety for Kids and Teens course is a free, online course that teaches children about internet safety, security, and responsible online behavior. It is available for both iOS and Android devices. Website: https://www.fbi.gov/resources/students-parents/internet-safety

By taking these courses, children can learn how to be safe online and develop responsible online habits.

The Dangers of Cyberbullying and How to Respond

Another important aspect of online safety is teaching kids about the dangers of cyberbullying and how to respond if they encounter it. Cyberbullying can include things like mean or threatening messages, harassment, or the sharing of embarrassing or private information. It can have serious consequences, including low self-esteem, depression, and even suicide.

To help prevent cyberbullying and protect kids from its effects, parents should teach kids to:

Ignore bullies and not engage with them: Kids should be taught to ignore bullies and not engage with them. This can help to prevent the situation from escalating and give the bully less power.

Report bullying to a trusted adult: If kids encounter cyberbullying, they should be encouraged to report it to a trusted adult, such as a parent or teacher. This can help to get the situation resolved and provide support to the victim.

Seek support from trusted friends and family: Kids who are being bullied online may feel isolated and alone. It's important for them to know that they have support from trusted friends and family, and to seek that support if they need it.

Tips for Spotting and Avoiding Online Scams and Fraud

Kids may also be at risk of falling victim to online scams or fraud. These can include things like phishing scams, in which perpetrators try to trick kids into giving out personal information, or fake online stores or contests that ask for payment or personal information. To help kids avoid these scams and protect themselves, parents should teach them to:

Be cautious about giving out personal information: Kids should be taught to be cautious about giving out personal information online, even if they are asked by someone they know. They should be encouraged to ask a trusted adult for advice before sharing personal information.

Look for red flags: Kids should also be taught to look for red flags that may indicate a scam or fraud, such as requests for payment or personal information, or offers that seem too good to be true.

Report suspicious activity to a trusted adult: If kids encounter a situation that seems suspicious or inappropriate, they should be encouraged to report it to a trusted adult. This can help to prevent them from falling victim to a scam or fraud.

By teaching kids to protect their personal information, discussing the dangers of cyberbullying and how to respond, and providing tips for spotting and avoiding online scams and fraud, parents can help to ensure that their kids are safer while they are online.

Chapter 5: Parental Controls and Monitoring Tools

To help parents keep track of their kids' online activities and protect them from potential risks, there are a variety of parental control and monitoring tools available. These tools can allow parents to set age-appropriate restrictions, block inappropriate content, and monitor their kids' online activities.

Overview of Parental Control Options

There are many different types of parental control tools available, each with its own set of features and capabilities. Some options include:

Device-level controls: Many devices, such as smartphones, tablets, and computers, offer built-in parental control features that allow parents to set age-appropriate restrictions, block inappropriate content, and monitor their kids' online activities. These controls can be accessed through the device's settings menu.

Internet service provider (ISP) controls: Some ISPs offer parental control features that allow parents to set limits on internet usage, block inappropriate content, and monitor their kids' online activities. These controls can be accessed through the ISP's online portal or app.

Browser-level controls: Some web browsers, such as Google Chrome and Mozilla Firefox, offer built-in parental control features that allow parents to block inappropriate websites, set time limits on internet usage, and monitor their kids' online activities. These controls can be accessed through the browser's settings menu.

Third-party apps and software: There are also a variety of third-party apps and software programs available that offer parental control features. These can include things like screen time management apps, content filtering tools, and monitoring software.

List of Computer Monitoring Applications

There are several Windows and Mac applications that feature parental controls, including:

Qustodio: Qustodio is a parental control app that allows parents to track their child's online activity, set limits on device usage, and block inappropriate websites and apps. It is available for both Windows and Mac devices.

Net Nanny: Net Nanny is a parental control app that allows parents to track their child's online activity, set limits on device usage, and block inappropriate websites and apps. It is available for both Windows and Mac devices.

Kaspersky Safe Kids: Kaspersky Safe Kids is a parental control app that allows parents to track their child's online activity, set limits on device usage, and block inappropriate websites and apps. It is available for both Windows and Mac devices.

By using these apps, parents can monitor their child's activities and help ensure that they are using their devices safely and responsibly.

Setting Up Parental Controls on Different Devices

To set up parental controls on different devices, parents will need to follow the specific instructions for each device or platform. Some general steps that may be involved include:

Connecting the device to a home network: To set up parental controls on a device, it will need to be connected to a home network. This can typically be done by connecting the device to the router via an Ethernet cable or by connecting to the router's wireless network.

Setting up a user account: Many devices and platforms require users to set up a user account in order to access certain features or content. Parents may need to create a user account for their kids in order to set up parental controls.

Configuring the parental control settings: Once a user account has been set up, parents can access the device's or platform's parental control settings and configure them as desired. This may involve setting age-appropriate restrictions, blocking inappropriate websites or apps, and setting limits on internet usage.

Tips for Using Monitoring Tools Effectively

To use monitoring tools effectively, parents should keep the following tips in mind:

Set clear expectations: Before using monitoring tools, parents should set clear expectations with their kids about what types of online activities are acceptable and what types are not. This can help to prevent misunderstandings and establish a sense of trust and transparency.

Use monitoring tools as a tool, not a crutch: Monitoring tools can be a helpful tool for keeping track of kids' online activities, but they should not be relied on as a replacement for communication and supervision. Parents should still make an effort to talk to their kids about their online activities and set limits on internet usage as appropriate.

Stay informed about new apps and platforms: The online landscape is constantly evolving, with new apps and platforms being introduced all the time. Parents should stay informed about these new developments and consider using monitoring tools to keep track of their kids' use of these platforms.

Use monitoring tools in combination with other strategies: Monitoring tools should be used in combination with other strategies for keeping kids safe online, such as setting limits on screen time, establishing age-appropriate restrictions, and teaching kids about internet safety.

Be aware of the potential drawbacks of monitoring tools: While monitoring tools can be helpful, they can also have some drawbacks. For example, they may invade kids' privacy or create a sense of mistrust between kids and their parents. It's important for parents to be aware of these potential drawbacks and use monitoring tools responsibly.

Use monitoring tools in an age-appropriate way: Parents should also be aware of the age-appropriateness of different monitoring tools and use them accordingly. For example, older kids may have more privacy concerns and may not want their parents to monitor their online activities as closely as younger kids.

By following these tips, parents can use monitoring tools effectively as part of their overall strategy for keeping their kids safe online.

Chapter 6: Responding to Online Incidents

As a parent, it is important to be prepared for the possibility that your child may encounter online incidents such as cyberbullying or inappropriate behavior. It can be difficult to know what to do in these situations, but taking the right steps can help to minimize the impact on your child and prevent future incidents from occurring.

Steps to Take if Your Child is a Victim of Cyberbullying

Listen to your child and believe what they are telling you. It is important to validate your child's feelings and experiences and let them know that you support them.

Document the incident. Save any harassing messages or posts and take screenshots if possible. This documentation can be helpful if you need to report the incident to school officials or law enforcement.

Help your child block the perpetrator. Most social media platforms have tools that allow you to block or report users who are engaging in harassing behavior.

Contact the perpetrator's parents or guardians. In some cases, it may be helpful to have a conversation with the parents or guardians of the person who is bullying your child. This can be a delicate situation, so it is important to approach it with care and respect.

Report the incident to the appropriate authorities. If the cyberbullying is severe or persistent, it may be necessary to report the incident to school officials or law enforcement.

Seek outside support. If your child is struggling with the effects of cyberbullying, it may be helpful to seek the support of a therapist or other mental health professional.

How to Handle Inappropriate Online Behavior

Set clear rules and boundaries for online behavior. It is important to establish rules and boundaries for your child's online activity, such as not sharing personal information or engaging in inappropriate conversations.

Monitor your child's online activity. Regularly checking in on your child's online activity can help you to identify any potential issues or concerns.

Use parental controls. Many devices and internet service providers offer tools that allow you to set limits on your child's online activity, such as blocking certain websites or setting time limits.

Educate your child about online safety. Help your child to understand the importance of being safe online and how to protect themselves from potential dangers.

Tips for Talking to Your Child About Online Incidents

Keep the conversation age-appropriate. Tailor your discussion to your child's age and understanding.

Emphasize that they can come to you with any concerns. It is important for your child to know that they can come to you with any problems or concerns they have about their online activity.

Focus on solutions. Instead of dwelling on the negative aspects of the incident, try to focus on ways to prevent similar incidents from happening in the future.

Encourage open and honest communication. Encourage your child to be open and honest with you about their online activity and any issues or concerns they may have.

Seek outside support if necessary. If your child is struggling to cope with the effects of an online incident, it may be helpful to seek the support of a therapist or other mental health professional.

By following these steps and tips, you can help your child to navigate online incidents and keep them safe and healthy in their online lives.

Chapter 7: Staying Up to Date

As technology and the internet continue to evolve, it is important for parents to stay up to date on the latest apps and platforms that their children may be using, as well as online safety issues that could potentially impact their children. In this chapter, we will discuss the importance of keeping track of new apps and platforms and staying informed about online safety issues.

Keeping Track of New Apps and Platforms

Stay vigilant: Be on the lookout for new apps and platforms that your children may be interested in using. It is important to be aware of the potential risks and dangers that these apps and platforms may pose, such as the possibility of cyberbullying or exposure to inappropriate content.

Research apps and platforms before allowing your child to use them: Take the time to research the app or platform before allowing your child to use it. Look for reviews and information about the app's privacy policies and safety features.

Set limits and establish rules: Consider setting limits on the amount of time your child is allowed to spend on apps and platforms, and establish rules for their use.

Have open and honest conversations with your child: Talk to your child about the apps and platforms they are using and encourage them to come to you with any concerns or questions they have.

Staying Informed About Online Safety Issues

Follow online safety resources and experts: Keep up to date on the latest online safety issues by following trusted resources and experts in the field. There are resources listed at the end of this book.

Educate yourself: Take the time to learn about online safety issues and how to protect your child from potential risks.

Educate your child: Enroll your child in an online safety course.

Communicate with your child: Have ongoing conversations with your child about online safety and encourage them to come to you with any concerns or questions they have.

Stay involved in your child's online activities: Regularly check in on your child's online activities and be proactive in addressing any potential issues that may arise.

By staying up to date on new apps and platforms and staying informed about online safety issues, you can help ensure that your child has a safe and positive online experience.

Chapter 8: Resources and Further Learning

Below are websites that offer resources for parents on how to keep their children safe online. By staying informed and taking proactive steps to protect their children, parents can help ensure that their kids have a safe and positive online experience.

Cybersecurity and Infrastructure Security Agency (CISA): CISA is a division of the Department of Homeland Security and provides resources on how to keep kids safe online, including tips on how to create strong passwords, protect personal information, and report cyberbullying.
https://www.cisa.gov/kids

Federal Bureau of Investigation (FBI): The FBI has a website dedicated to internet safety for kids, with information on topics such as cyberbullying, sexting, and online predators.
https://www.fbi.gov/scams-and-safety/internet-safety

National Center for Missing & Exploited Children (NCMEC): NCMEC is a nonprofit organization that works to prevent child abduction and sexual exploitation. The organization offers resources for parents on how to keep kids safe online, including information on internet safety, cyberbullying, and online predators.
https://www.missingkids.org/theissues/internet-safety

StopBullying.gov: This website, which is managed by the U.S. Department of Health and Human Services, provides information and resources on bullying prevention, including cyberbullying.
https://www.stopbullying.gov/cyberbullying/what-is-it

U.S. Department of Education: The U.S. Department of Education offers resources for parents on how to keep kids safe online, including information on internet safety, cyberbullying, and online predators. https://www2.ed.gov/about/offices/list/oese/oshs/safe.html

I sincerely hope this book has been helpful in your journey to protect your children online. I call this a *journey* because as with all technology, things are always changing and evolving. It's important to stay on top of new information as no book or resource can cover everything nor stay current. The websites above can help you stay informed and educated, as well as your local news channels and websites, and community resources.

Made in the USA
Columbia, SC
28 January 2023